Originally published as *De tandarts* in Belgium and the Netherlands by Clavis Uitgeverij, 2017
English translation from the Dutch by Clavis Publishing Inc., New York

Copyright © 2017 Clavis Publishing Inc., New York

Visit us on the Web at www.clavis-publishing.com.

Dentists and What They Do (small size edition) written and illustrated by Liesbet Slegers

ISBN 978-1-60537-385-0

This book was printed in April 2022 at Graspo CZ, a.s.,
Pod Šternberkem 324, 76302 Zlín, Czech Republic.

First Edition
10 9 8 7 6 5 4 3

Dentists
and What They Do

Liesbet Slegers

Clavis

NEW YORK

Look! My mouth is full of teeth.
I brush them every day.
But sometimes the dentist checks them for me.

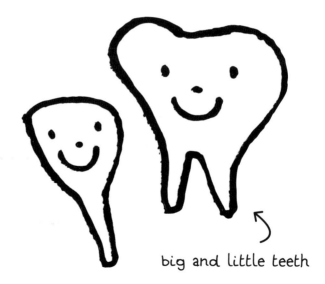

big and little teeth

The dentist wears a white coat
and plastic gloves.
She puts a mask over her mouth
when she looks at my teeth.

how funny!

mask

plastic gloves

white coat

The dentist has many tools
to check my teeth and clean them.
She feels my teeth with a probe
and uses a mirror to look at the back of my mouth.

rinse,
please!

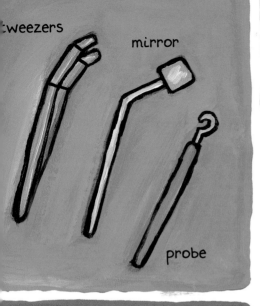

tweezers

mirror

probe

light

tissues

soap

dentist's chair

The dentist tells me what's good for my teeth.
After having a snack, I should drink a glass of water
and rinse my mouth clean.

I have my own toothbrush and toothpaste at home. I brush my teeth in the morning and again at night.
That way, my teeth can rest overnight.
Sleep tight, teeth!

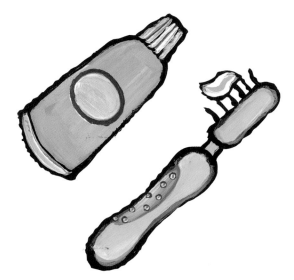

brush well!

I'm going to visit the dentist.
First the dentist checks my stuffed animal's teeth.
"Aha! He's brushed properly," she says. "Well done!"

my stuffed
animal

Now I open my mouth wide
so that the dentist can take a good look.
Using her little mirror she can even see
the big teeth all the way at the back.

shine, shine

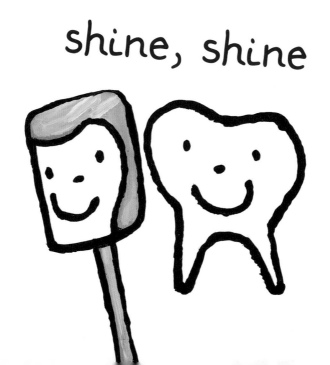

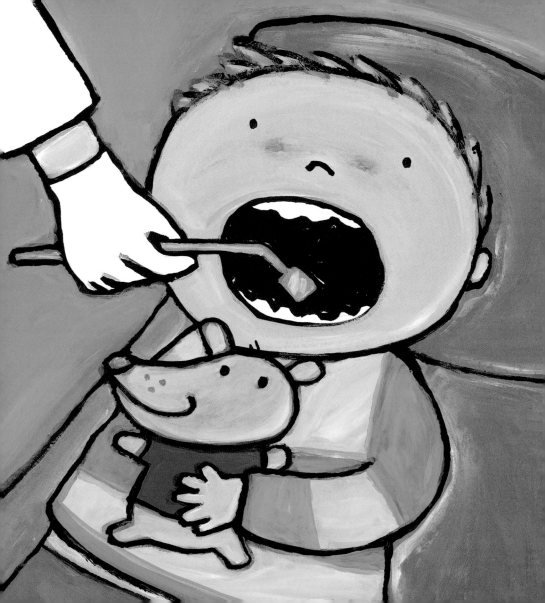

The dentist looks at my teeth.
Sometimes she touches them with a probe.
That feels strange!
It's like a tiny gnome tickling my teeth.

tickle,
tickle

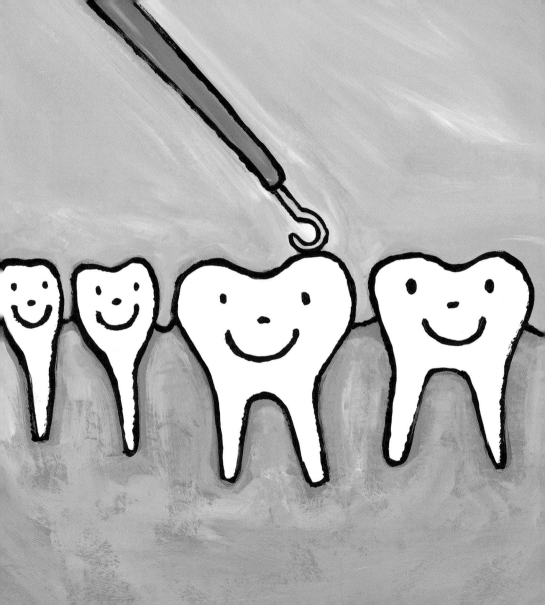

Then the dentist takes a photo of my teeth.
Are there any holes?
Are the new teeth ready to come in?
That's funny! A tooth photo!

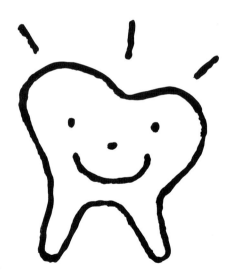

"You've been brushing well," says the dentist.
"Everything looks good!"
Hooray! I have a healthy mouth with strong teeth.
"Bravo!" says Mommy.

okay!

The dentist gives me a tube of kids' toothpaste.
There's a bunny on the tube.
That will make brushing even more fun.
Goodbye! See you next time!

This wheel shows what's good for your toddler's teeth.
(A balanced diet is very important.)
Let your child describe what they see on the wheel.